# Cogency:

## Discover Easy And Proven Methods Of Manipulation

**Disclamer:** All photos used in this book, including the cover photo were made available under a Attribution-NonCommercial-ShareAlike 2.0 Generic and sourced from Flickr

Table of content

## Introduction

You think you are in control of what you are doing today. You are going to get ready for work, you are going to head out the door, and you are going to work your job until it is time to go home.

After you leave your work, you are going to get your errands done, perhaps run by the grocery store, and go home to do the things you do every evening. Sure, you think you are on top of your game, but there's not much happening in your day to day life.

If you really think about it, you are stuck in the same cycle, doing the same thing over and over. You don't change much, though you want change, and you don't try to do much, because you are scared to get out of your comfort zone. As a result, nothing really happens in your life besides the same old, same old.

Now, you can change all of that. You can take control of your life and head down a path that is going to lead you to success. You don't have to worry anymore that you won't get the promotion you want. Or that you won't get the job you want.

You can forget about worrying about that date, because you already know it is going to go well and you will get a second one. You don't need to worry about your money problems, your organizational skills, or anything.

Now, you are able to take control of your life, and you are able to change your luck. This boos is going to be your handy guide in the art of persuasion and success. I know how to do this because I have done it. I know how you can change your life for the better, starting today!

And this isn't going to be something that is hit and miss. This isn't going to be left up to chance anymore. This isn't going to be that stressful hope you cling to without any real cause. This is going to be real advice that gives you real results.

So are you ready to take control of your life and dominate lady luck? Are you ready to step out of the world of "happenstance" and move into the world that you can control?

This book is going to change your life.

So let's get started.

## Chapter 1 – Turn Your Luck Around

So many people view themselves as a victim of circumstance. They think that life is out to get them and they have been dealt a bad hand. There are those that are the "lucky" ones, and there are the rest of us.

Does this sound familiar?

Well, I want to change that around for you.

You don't have to be a victim of circumstance anymore. You don't have to wonder if things are going to work out for you, and you don't have to wish for the best. If you know how to walk the walk and talk the talk, you really can have control over many of the situations you run into in your life.

### How?

The answer is really straight forward. Many of the situations we find ourselves in are situations that arise from our own actions. You and everyone else around you reacts and interacts in certain ways. However, you may be doing things that are causing reactions you don't want to have.

You may be causing minor offenses without even realizing it, and you may be taking offense at things you shouldn't be. You react to situations the way you are viewing them, but unless you have a deeper understanding about what is going on, you are only living in reactions.

Now, the issue that lies in living in reactions is that you must always recoil and recover from a given situation. I don't want you to have to do this anymore. In fact, I want you to have actual control over the various situations that arise during your day, and have a hand in the outcome.

The secret to doing this lies in your ability to read people.

If you only drift through your day without taking any real action, you are left to respond to how the people around you are acting. This can lead to problems since you may or may not be responding to them in the right way.

*For example:*

*You are having a conversation with a friend through text message. Through the course of the conversation, you end up saying something you meant as a joke. Your friend says something back to you that offends you.*

*Before you know it, you are in a heated conversation that went very wrong, without even being certain as to why you are arguing in the first place.*

You may think the reason you are arguing with your friend is because of what they said, but the real reason you are arguing is because of your reaction to what they said. After all, they may have meant it one way or another... in a way that is entirely different than what you took it as.

And this problem arises again and again throughout your day without you even realizing it. You are constantly responding to situations based on your understating of that situation, and others are doing the same with you.

**But how do I use this knowledge to change my luck?**

Your luck or good fortune is in reality largely based on how you are responding to the situations around you, and vice versa. If you want to change your luck, you need to change the way you respond to these situations.

Once you are able to keep your reaction to any situation under control, and better project your own feelings to those around you, you are going to see your luck do a complete turnaround.

The secret to all of this lies in the little skill I like to call body language.

Body language is the way you say what you really mean without ever saying a word. You can tell the world how you feel, and you can see how someone else is feeling all based on their body language.

When you master the art of reading and speaking body language, you are going to erase any of the issues you have ever had in your day. You will be able to project and respond in ways you never realized you could, and as a result you are going to watch your luck change.

Let me show you how you can make this difference in your life, and what you can do starting right now to start changing that luck.

The results are real, and so is your luck.

## Chapter 2 – Persuasion Part One: The Art of Reading People

When you want to turn your luck around, the first thing you need to do is change the people around you. After all, everything that you consider to be lucky or unlucky is based on your interactions with other people.

Whether you want to get that promotion at work, snag that date, or grab that sweet deal, you need to have great interactions with people. You may think that people skills have nothing to do with this, but think about it for a second.

You walk over to that pretty girl over there, and you work your skills. You do your best, but you end up being turned down, which you then blame on having bad luck.

But wait a second.

Suppose your alleged "bad luck" was actually poor people skills. Perhaps even though you were doing your best to get that date, you actually sent the wrong impression which is what caused her to turn you down?

You may think you have this all figured out, but that may not be true. In all actuality if you want to change your luck, you have to change how you are interaction with the people around you.

**Read to respond**

Before you can know what you should do in an interaction, you have to know what is going on in that interaction. If you have no clue how the other person is responding, you can't possibly know how you should act to make the situation work out in your favor.

So, let's make this work. Let's take a look at the most obvious (yet subtle) signs people project on a daily basis, and what you can do to in response to these signs to turn the situation in your favor.

*Let's start with the list of negatives. These are the things people do when they are feeling impatient, insecure, or like they don't want to be in that situation.*

*If you see someone doing this, you are annoying them, boring them, or aggravating them. This is when you know you need to change up your game plan.*

- They look around the room while you are speaking
- They are tapping their feet or drumming their hands or fingers on anything
- Heavy sighs, changing the subject, or asking you to repeat yourself
- General agitation, disinterest, or checking their phone or watch

In other words, if you are trying to have a conversation with someone, and they are doing any of these things, you aren't giving them what they need in the interaction. You need to change it up, and gain their interest back.

You can do this in a number of ways, but the fastest and easiest way to do this is to make the conversation about them. Ask them something. Ask about what they are wearing, what they are working on, or some achievement you know of.

In any way you can, make the conversation about them, and not about you. This is the fastest way to bring their attention back to the present, because everyone loves to talk about themselves.

*On the other hand, there are definite signs you have someone's attention. If you see any of these things, you know you are on the right track and have their full attention.*

- They are focused on you as you are talking

- They are facing you in some way, even if it is just with their feet or arms

- Eye contact. Lots and lots of eye contact

- They are talking about the same subject you are, without trying to change it

It is a pretty obvious thing when someone isn't interested in you or what you are talking about.

Your goal is to capture the attention of the world around you first and foremost. When you do this, you are then better able to gauge your actions based on what your audience is doing.

**Okay, great, but how is that going to help me change my luck around?**

I know reading body language doesn't seem like it has much to do with your luck, but trust me, it does.

Think of the people you know that just seem to have the greatest luck of anyone around them. Now, think of what these people have in common.

Is it looks?

Is it where they live or what they drive?

Is it who they are?

No, it's not of these things. What it is in reality is the fact that they know how to work situations to their own advantage. They know how to get people to do what they want, and they can do this by their ability to read body language.

In this chapter, you need to practice your own ability to read the world around you, but in the next chapter, I am going to show you how this all applies to what you are doing. When you are able to use your skills to your advantage, you are going to see your luck change.

## Chapter 3 – Persuasion Part 2: Influence

I wish I could say all you needed to do was know how to read people, but in reality, that is only half the fun. Once you are able to influence the world around you, you will find that influence is one of the most fun things you can do.

You don't have to stress about how a situation is going to turn out, because you know how it is going to turn out. You know that when you walk into a situation, you are going to walk out of it ahead of where you were when you entered the situation.

Now, let's get into the thick of it, and learn how you can influence people to your benefit.

***The key is to get the people around you to want to do what you want. When you are able to seamlessly make your way seem like their idea, you are in the perfect place to get your way, and make your luck change.***

So what should you do to make everyone believe that your way is the only way? Here are the few things that are going to make you the star of the show every time:

- Be confident – in other words, don't be afraid to be embarrassed. In fact, don't even allow yourself to feel embarrassment. Life happens, and the same funny things happen to everyone, so when something happens to you, let it roll off your back.

On the other hand, let your confidence shine out and embrace life as it comes. The more you are able to do this, the more people are going to be attracted to you.

- Make everything about the other person, while you are making it about you – you have your ideas, and you know what you want done, but if you want to get other people to go along with it, you need to make them think it's their idea.

To do this, you need to highlight the points from your idea that benefit them, and use those points to convince them to go along with your idea.

*For example:*

*You know you want that promotion at work, so you need to highlight your skills to your boss. Let your boss know that you have the skills they need in that opening, but make sure you just let your boss know that you have those skills.*

*If you highlight the skills, your boss is going to think of the situation objectively, and focus on how it benefits the company as a whole. Going along with this idea, your boss is going to give you the promotion you want, but they are going to think that it is their idea as they do it.*

*So you see, you got your way, and you changed your own luck as you did, but you made your boss think that it was his idea the entire time.*

*You can use this skill when it comes to all kinds of situations in life, so long as you are able to make your way their idea, you are in.*

- Be positive – everyone likes the positive person, so the more you are able to point out the good, the more people are going to want to be around you. For as much as people complain, they really do like that person that is positive. It is something that is born into all of us.

- Be open – when you are interacting with the world around you, you need to be open. Never cross your arms as you are speaking with someone, and don't look down at them or away from them.

  Keep eye contact as much as you comfortably can, and keep the focus on them, even when you are talking about yourself. I know this is going to be a bit of a challenge at first, but the more you are able to focus on the world around you, the more people are going to focus on you, and the more they are going to want to be a part of what you are doing.

These are skills you need to master if you want to influence the world around you. It is the combination of reading the people with whom you are speaking, as well as speaking to them in ways that they don't realize you are.

Influence is a silent way of communicating, and it is something that does take practice if you want to master it in the long run. You see, you may have had some interactions already that turned out in your favor that you think were just luck, but in reality you were doing something that made the other people want to give you your way.

This is something that is going to take time to recognize in your day to day life, but the more you practice looking for it, the more it is going to become evident to you.

## Chapter 4 – Using Silence to Say Everything

The more you learn about influence, persuasion, and your ability to change your own luck, you are going to notice that you really don't need to say much to make all of this happen. There are a lot of times in life when nothing at all is the best thing to say, and knowing when those moments arrive is crucial in your quest for success.

The first thing I want to address is when you should opt for silence in an interaction. In order to have the best influence on the world around you, you need to know when you should stop talking. I know this sounds funny when you are first starting out, but trust me on this.

The life of the party and the confident person are two different people. We think that the person with the most to say, with the loudest way of saying it, and who is always looking to be the center of attention is the person with confidence, but in reality, this is the person with the least amount of confidence.

Anyone that knows what true confidence really is will laugh at the person that craves being the center of attention. They know that the person that is truly confident doesn't need the validation from the world around them to tell them that they are confident.

So, if you want to attract the people around you to yourself, you have to know when to speak, and when to keep silent.

Here are a few rules of thumb to keep you in line. Keep them in mind whenever you are in a situation when you don't know if you should speak or not, and watch the amazing results that follow!

1. **Never speak just to fill the space**

   When there is a promotion on the line, and you don't know who is going to get it, don't be the person that is annoying. Don't just talk for the sake of talking, because you never know who is listening in on it, and you don't know where it's going to lead.

2. **Never join in on gossip**

   Gossip may seem like fun at the time, but again, you never know who is going to say what, or who is going to hear it. It is incredibly easy to ruin your chances at a lot of things in life if you just join in on a little gossip... and believe me, it isn't worth the trouble for the little bit of rumor.

3. **Never make off color or racist jokes**

   One of the best ways to change your luck is to gain respect. You don't think of the person whom nobody respects as the person who is making it big in life.

   It is the person with respect that is the person who has good luck. If you make off colored jokes you may be getting a few laughs at the time, but you aren't getting the respect of the people around you, and this could greatly harm you in the long run.

### 4. **Never talk about people**

That's really all I need to say about this one. There's never any reason for it, so don't do it. Ever. If you refuse to talk about the people around you, then you are going to gain a lot of respect with people as a whole, because they know you won't discuss it with others.

This is going to work out to your advantage in the long run, because people will choose you for the things you want to be chosen for.

### 5. **Always give your true and honest opinion, even when it isn't popular**

You may think that saying what people want to hear is the way to go when you are trying to gain the respect of people, but that's not the case. If you want to get the biggest following, even if it is just a social following, you need to be up front and honest.

There are a lot of times in life when you don't know how you should respond to what is going on, and a lot of times, we opt to say things we shouldn't and we opt to say things that will just hopefully make us popular.

But, if you want to change your luck, you need to say the right things that will land you in with the crowd you want to be in with, and to do this you need to stay on the upside of the rules.

I know it can be hard, and it will make for a few awkward moments, but with practice, you are going to know just what to say any place, and any time. This is going to take you up on the scale of respect as well as success, and you will watch your luck change right alongside.

## Chapter 5 – Five Essential Steps to Living the Lucky Life

It's funny to think how few things actually have to do with you when it comes to your own luck. Essentially, if you want to be lucky, you have to learn how to relate to and interact with the world around you, and let this lead you to the success you want to have.

This is going to take some practice, but I know you are going to be able to get it down as second nature if you work at it.

While these things are important, there are a few more things you need to remember if you want to be successful and change your luck for good.

Here are the five essential things lucky people do.

1. **Feel your own power**

   If you understand that you are powerful, you will act like you are. Before you go into anything, you need to stand up tall, and act like you are powerful. If you do this, you are going to feel powerful, and as a result you are going to act powerful.

2. **Believe in your own power**

You can look and act as powerful as you wish, but unless you believe that you are powerful, you aren't going to treat situations like you should.

As you go through your day, act like you believe you are powerful, and you will be treated like you are.

### 3. Be the leader people can follow

If you think you are a leader, people are going to follow you. People want to follow, it's just in our nature. If you are a person that believes you should be followed, you are going to get that following.

As a result, your ideas are going to be listened to, and you are going to get your way a lot more. The more you get your way, the more you are going to see your luck change.

It is the combination of knowing that you have good ideas and being willing to put them out into the world that is going to get you the results you want in the long run.

### 4. Speak clearly in life about what you want

The number one thing you need to accept in life is the fact that people can't read your mind. This means if you want something, you have to say clearly what you want and follow up on it.

Don't simply sit back and hope that people will follow you just because, you need to put out there what you want and show people that is what they should do.

When you are able to do this, you are going to get the results that you want in the long run, and you will see your luck change.

## 5. Refuse to be defeated

Another thing you need to remember is the fact that you don't have to give up. Things are going to happen that are good, and things are going to happen that are bad.

You are going to get your way at times, and you are going to run into problems at other times. The main thing you need to do is remember that just because you don't get your way it doesn't mean that you aren't lucky.

There are times when you need to step back and re-evaluate what is going on, and go from there. Perhaps you are going to have to change things up to get the end goal you are after, and the so called bad luck is going to end up luckier than you would have been otherwise.

Luck isn't nearly as elusive as you would think it is. A large part of the luck you see in the world is the result of a lot of hard work, and the lucky people that you know are skilled at getting what they want based on things they know. When you know how to handle the world around you, you are going to see the same things happen in your own life.

Lady luck isn't as hard to get along with as you would think, you just have to know what you are doing. I want you to be successful, and I want you to be as lucky as you want to be. If you follow the rules in this book, and if you are willing to stick with it through the easy times as well as the hard, you are going to get the results you want and see the luck grow in your life.

Soon, this is all going to be such second nature to you that you won't even realize that you weren't always so lucky. You are going to see what you want, and you are going to go for it, then you are going to get it. This way of life has an avalanche affect. The more you work at it, the more it will grow, and the better it is going to be.

Luck is something that everyone can have, including you. It has nothing to do with your job, where you live, or who you are. If you want to be a lucky person, get out there and make yourself lucky!

You got this.

# Conclusion

There you have it! Everything you need to know to change your life for the better. Now you don't have to stress that your life is headed in the right direction. You don't have to worry whether or not you are making the right choices, and you can eliminate the need to get the approval of everyone around you.

Remember that the next step is to stick with this, and to look the world in the eye and refuse to be beaten down. You know you are going to have good days, and you know you are going to have bad days. We all do, and we always will.

The key is to not let the bad days get you down, or to let fear run your life. With the skills I have outlined in this book, you are going to be able to change your luck for the better, guaranteed!

I know this can be scary at first, but I really want to shake that fear out of you and let you live the life of freedom you have been craving. You were designed to take life by the horns, and you were meant to be happy. With that in mind, forget all of this worry, forget how you let fear control you, and forget the negativity that tries to take hold of your life.

When you do this, you are taking control of your own life, and you are going to see those results you wish to see.

Good luck!

www.ingramcontent.com/pod-product-compliance
Lightning Source LLC
Chambersburg PA
CBHW070023260726
48658CB00003B/1019